DECODING ANGEL NUMBERS

A SPIRITUAL GUIDE TO DIVINE MESSAGES TO CONNECT WITH THE UNIVERSE THROUGH NUMBERS AND NUMEROLOGY

STEVEN W. WATSON

Editing Software with AI
GRAMMARLY PRO

Disclaimer

The content of this book is intended for educational and informational purposes only. The interpretations and meanings of angel numbers, including master numbers, are based on spiritual beliefs and numerological systems that may vary among individuals and traditions. This book is not intended to provide professional advice, and readers should use their own discretion when applying the insights shared. The information provided should not be used as a substitute for professional counselling, financial, medical, or legal services. Any actions taken as a result of reading this book are solely the responsibility of the reader.

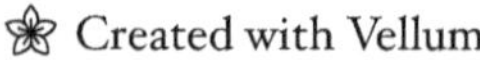 Created with Vellum

CONTENTS

Introduction   5

Brief Introduction to Angel Numbers   9
How to use this book   13
What is Spirituality?   17
What is Meditation?   21
What is Intuition?   31
Role of Guardian Angels and Spirit
Guides   37
Origin of Angel Numbers   41
What are Master Numbers   45
Numerology   53
000   59
111   63
222   67
333   71
444   75
555   79
666   83
777   87
888   91
999   97
1111   101
1010   105
1212   113
What are Pattern Numbers?   117
What to do When You Encounter Angel
Numbers   123
Conclusion   129

About the Author   131

INTRODUCTION

Welcome to the incredible journey of life on Earth! When we arrive here, we carry a sense of amnesia, temporarily forgetting our origins and purpose. However, as we navigate life, we are presented with valuable spiritual growth and learning opportunities. If you take a moment to pause and reflect, you'll discover that each of us is here to embrace the lessons we've chosen for ourselves through our higher selves. This profound experience serves as a guiding light, offering insights into the reasons behind our chosen lessons and how they contribute to the evolution of our souls.

Our souls originate from diverse and fascinating places. Some of us have deep connections to Earth, while others are the embodiments of beings from distant galaxies or alternate dimensions. We can uncover remarkable insights about ourselves through meditation, spiritual practices, and connecting with our spirit guides and team. It's crucial to remain open to the synchronicities in our lives. For example, a chance encounter with a stranger might unexpectedly solve a long-standing question, liberating us from a cycle of uncertainty. Sometimes, specific song lyrics come to us immediately, offering profound guidance.

Additionally, many people notice repeating numbers, each carrying personal significance and serving as powerful guides - these are angel numbers. While these numbers have established meanings, you can also interpret them uniquely. One approach is to record the sequences of numbers you encounter and assign them personal meanings, creating a personalized communication system with your spirit team.

BRIEF INTRODUCTION TO ANGEL NUMBERS

I constantly encounter angel numbers, whether at work, enjoying personal time, or out in public. The universe speaks to me through these sequences, and my family is often amazed by how frequently they appear. I also receive messages through music, whether from the songs playing around me or from an inner "DJ" who selects the perfect song for me or someone nearby, offering the necessary message of what is needed at that moment.

BEFORE WE DELVE DEEPER, let's take a moment to understand angel numbers. Where do they come from, what do they mean, and why do they seem to follow some people more than others?

. . .

IN NUMEROLOGY, angel numbers are sequences of numbers, often appearing in groups of three or four and featuring repeated digits or distinct patterns. They have a remarkable way of capturing our attention and evoking a sense of wonder by appearing in unexpected places, such as on a clock, a passing license plate, or a receipt. These numbers are believed to carry deeper meanings, resonating with energies that transcend the physical realm.

THE ALLURE of angel numbers lies in their symbolism. Many believe these sequences are direct messages from the spiritual universe—whether from higher powers, angels, spirit guides, or even our subconscious minds—offering wisdom, clarity, and insight during significant moments in life. They may appear when facing a difficult decision, navigating a challenge, or simply needing reassurance that we're on the right path.

ANGEL NUMBERS ARE like nudges from the universe, helping us figure out the repeating patterns and moments in our lives. By noticing when and how they appear, we can decode secret messages and better understand our path. Whether you see them as spiritual hints or echoes of our thoughts, angel numbers illuminate the mundane and magical moments, giving us those much-needed insights when needed.

. . .

As you explore these numbers, you may ask why they follow you and what they mean. I've developed my interpretation of these numbers through years of exploration, research, and learning. You can use my insights as a guide or create your system of meanings that resonates with your unique connection to the universe, your ancestors, higher consciousness, ascended masters, angels, or even God if that aligns with your beliefs. After all, these are your messages from the universe. Some have even said to create a list of what these numbers mean to you, a cheat sheet to your spirit guides for a personal message invoked from them.

HOW TO USE THIS BOOK

I am glad you asked. This book is about how to connect with spirituality, your intuition and the numbers themselves. Take what is given here as a root for your exploration. You can use the definitions that have been provided or use them as gentle guidance to your interpretation of the meanings of what you have for yourself. There is no right or wrong way to use this book, just as long as it resonates with you. With that, I hope you enjoy the information I have compiled here and wish you the best on your journey of self-discovery.

WHEN YOU ENCOUNTER the angel numbers, they act as a guidebook for you to flip to the page and read about the number you encountered. It is recommended that you journal your experience, including what thoughts you might have had, the energy that you were experiencing, and any relevant facts. This will help you interpret the numbers that you have seen.

WHAT IS SPIRITUALITY?

Spirituality is a broad concept that involves a sense of connection to something greater than yourself. It often includes searching for meaning in life and can encompass beliefs, values, practices, and experiences related to the divine, source or the universe. While closely related to religion, spirituality is not confined to any specific religious tradition; it can be deeply personal and individualized.

At its core, spirituality is about exploring questions of existence: Why are we here? What is our purpose? What connects us to the universe and each other? It often involves seeking personal growth, inner peace, and a deeper understanding of life.

. . .

ESSENTIAL ELEMENTS OF SPIRITUALITY:

CONNECTION: Many spiritual traditions emphasize connecting with others, nature, or a higher power (God, source, the universe, et cetera – whatever feels suitable for you). This sense of connection can foster feelings of unity, compassion, and empathy.

TRANSCENDENCE: Spirituality often involves transcending the everyday experiences of life to find deeper meaning and experiencing something beyond the material world. This can be through meditation, prayer, or contemplation.

MEANING AND PURPOSE: Spirituality provides individuals with a sense of meaning and purpose in life. It helps people navigate difficult times, offering comfort and a framework for understanding life's challenges.

INNER EXPERIENCE: Spirituality often focuses on inner experiences and developing one's soul or inner self. This may involve practices that promote self-awareness, mindfulness, and personal reflection.

. . .

SPIRITUALITY VS. RELIGION:

WHILE RELIGION typically involves organized principles, rituals, and communal worship, spirituality can be more fluid and personal. People can be spiritual without religion, meaning they may seek meaning and connection outside traditional religious structures. Many religious people also embrace spirituality as a core part of their faith.

TYPES OF SPIRITUAL PRACTICES:

SPIRITUALITY CAN MANIFEST in a variety of ways, such as:
- *Meditation and mindfulness*
- *Prayer and worship*
- *Yoga and physical movement*
- *Journaling and self-reflection*
- *Nature walks and immersion in the natural world*

IN CONCLUSION, spirituality is a profoundly personal and diverse aspect of human life. It focuses on meaning, connection, and personal growth. It transcends specific religious practices and can be experienced in many ways, depending on your beliefs and life experiences.

WHAT IS MEDITATION?

*M*editation is much more than just a spiritual ritual; it's a journey toward mental clarity, emotional stability, and an oasis of inner peace. Imagine it as a gentle pause in the hustle of life, a moment to reconnect with the essence of being. It's not solely anchored in religious traditions but serves as a universal tool for enhancing personal well-being, easing stress, and fostering mental health.

THE BEAUTY of meditation is its inclusivity; it warmly welcomes everyone without concern for one's faith or physical capacity. Whether you prefer to meditate in a serene seated posture, lie down in comfort, or walk through nature, meditation moulds itself to fit into your life seamlessly.

. . .

FOR THOSE VENTURING into the world of meditation, a wealth of guided practices awaits to guide you through enriching experiences. And for individuals with aphantasia—a unique condition affecting 1 to 4% of the population characterized by the inability to visualize mental images—meditation remains equally accessible. Traditional guided meditations, emphasizing visual imagery, might pose challenges, but the essence of meditation transcends visualization, embracing various pathways to tranquillity.

DIVING into the core elements of meditation:

FOCUS: It's about channelling your attention to a singular point—the rhythm of your breath, a resonating sound, or the subtle sensations coursing through your body. This focus acts as an anchor, quieting the mind's chatter.

AWARENESS: Meditation invites an open-hearted awareness of your thoughts, emotions, and sensations, fostering a non-judgmental space where you can observe and release them, akin to leaves floating down a stream.

. . .

CALMNESS: The practice cultivates a profound sense of serenity and mastery over the mind's turbulence, reducing stress and anxiety and ushering in a calm state.

EXPLORING different meditation styles can enrich your practice of meditation:

MINDFULNESS MEDITATION: Rooted in the present, this practice encourages a conscious observation of your thoughts and emotions, letting them drift by without attachment or effort to alter them.

FOCUSED MEDITATION: Here, your attention is laser-focused on a chosen object, sound, or sensation. When distractions arise, gently guide your focus back, re-centering your mind.

LOVING-KINDNESS MEDITATION: This practice nurtures compassion and love towards oneself and others, expanding this benevolent energy to embrace all beings.

BODY SCAN MEDITATION: Journey through your body, from head to toe, tuning into areas of tension or discomfort and inviting relaxation. This method enhances body awareness and connection.

EMBRACING meditation is like opening the door to a realm of peace within, a sanctuary accessible to all, regardless of life's circumstances or personal challenges. It's a testament to the power of introspection and the boundless potential for transformation that lies within each of us.

HOW TO MEDITATE (EVEN if You Can't Visualize):

STEP 1: Find a Comfortable Position. This could be sitting in a chair with your feet firmly on the ground. You could choose to sit cross-legged. I meditate by lying flat on my back with my arms by my side. Remember that the aim isn't to fall asleep but rather to stay awake and be alert. You'll want to keep your back straight, relaxed, and able to breathe freely and easily. If you're sitting or crosslegged, look to keep your hands rested on your lap or knees.

STEP 2 (If it's comfortable for you): Close your eyes to eliminate distractions. If you don't find it comfortable to do so, find a fixed place to put your gaze.

. . .

Step 3: Focus on your breathing. Breath work is important here; you'll want to focus on the air as it moves freely through your nose, noticing the rise and fall of your chest and abdomen. However, if you need help focusing, try counting each inhale and exhale. For example, take a breath in; that's one; release that breath; that's two. Repeat until you feel settled.

Step 4: Noticing your thoughts. I get it; your mind will wander when you're trying to meditate. This is normal and okay. With these thoughts, like earlier said, you want to see them like passing clouds. Sometimes, the thoughts can be persistent. When this occurs, I acknowledge the thought, be grateful for it, and let it go. With that, I can return to my meditation. It is not about analyzing the thoughts or engaging deeply with them; it's more about letting them go, noticing they are there, but being present and focused on your breathing.

Step 5: Be present. If you are following a guided meditation and it's telling you to visualize, you aren't able to. That is okay. Don't worry; nothing is wrong with you. You choose to focus on a different thing. Sometimes, as I do have aphantasia, I tend to focus on things I can feel and relate to. It can be your breathing, body feeling, and sounds around you. The smallest sensory detail can help you be grounded and present during meditation.

STEP 6: Only try to run a marathon if you have learnt to walk. You can start with a shorter session. Start with 5 minutes. Gradually increase your length to 10, 15, 20, or as many minutes as you find helpful.

STEP 7: Do so with kindness when ready to end your meditation. Gently bring attention to your body and slowly transition from meditation to your surroundings. Take deep breaths and slowly open your eyes if they were closed. Acknowledge how your body feels before you get up.

SOME TIPS for Meditating Without Visualization:

USE PHYSICAL SENSATIONS: If you have trouble imagining or visualizing, focus on what you can feel. Notice the way your feet press against the floor, the weight of your hands, or the sensation of your clothing against your skin.

. . .

LISTEN TO SOUNDS: Pay attention to the sounds around you, whether it's the hum of a fan, distant traffic, or birds outside. Let the sounds anchor you without getting caught up in thinking about them. I recommend solfeggio frequencies to friends and family and enjoy myself. These are a set of a specific tone (frequency) believed to have healing properties and positive effects on the body and mind. Different frequencies, such as 396, 417, 528, 639, 741, 852 and 963 Hz, have various benefits per frequency. They're fascinating. If you don't know them and want to know more about them, I recommend looking them up and researching them.

FOCUS ON SIMPLE REPETITION: If focusing on your breath is challenging, you can silently repeat a simple word or phrase, like "calm" or "peace." The repetition can help keep your attention steady.

HERE ARE some benefits of meditation:

Stress reduction is a well-known effect of meditation. Meditation helps calm the nervous system and promote relaxation.

Through regulation meditation, you can enhance your ability to concentrate, helping you focus better on your daily activities.

Meditation can help reduce negative emotions like anxiety and anger. It can also help promote a more balanced mood. Self-awareness can also be known to increase as well.

Some studies have shown that regular meditation can help lower blood pressure, improve sleep, and enhance immune function.

To sum up, meditation is a practice of focused awareness that fosters relaxation, mental clarity, and emotional calm. You don't need to visualize or imagine anything during meditation (this is good if you have aphantasia like myself)—simply focusing on your breath, body sensations, or sounds can help you cultivate mindfulness and presence. With regular practice, meditation can enhance both mental and physical well-being.

WHAT IS INTUITION?

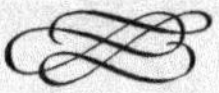

We all have this special something inside us, that gut feeling or that quiet voice in our head that nudges us when we're about to make a decision, even if we don't have all the facts laid out neatly in front of us. It's like having a sense when something feels just right or slightly off, without having to meticulously list the pros and cons. Think of it as your mind's own secret superpower, drawing from your past experiences, emotions, or those fleeting thoughts you weren't fully aware of to help guide you at life's various crossroads. This inner compass of ours might be more pronounced or easier to tune into for some, but it's an incredible tool to lean on when facing the unknown.

INTUITION SHOWS up differently for everyone: it could be that little "gut feeling" about a situation, a wave of unease when making tough decisions, or an unexpected flash of inspiration for a new idea. It acts like an inner guide, often without a clear explanation. Trying to describe intuition is like trying to describe the warmth of sunlight on your skin - it's a familiar sensation, yet hard to put into words.

LET'S dive into the intriguing world of intuition, exploring concepts like Clairvoyance, Clairaudience, Clairsentience, and Claircognizance.

CLAIRVOYANCE, OR "CLEAR SEEING," is an intuitive ability that lets some people gather information about an object, person, place, or event without using their five basic senses. It's as if they can see beyond the immediate, tangible world, accessing images of the past, present, or future. These images might appear in the mind's eye as vivid pictures, colors, symbols, or even scenes unfolding like a movie. Those with clairvoyant abilities might receive these insights out of the blue or by focusing their intention, helping them make decisions or understand situations on a deeper level. It's one way individuals can experience a unique connection to the unseen.

. . .

CLAIRAUDIENCE, OFTEN DESCRIBED AS "CLEAR HEARING," is the intuitive ability to receive messages or information through sound that isn't physically present. It's like tuning into a spiritual radio station, where you might hear voices, music, or even subtle sounds that guide you. These messages could come from spirit guides, angels, or higher realms, offering insight or wisdom. For many, clairaudience can feel like an inner voice or mental sound rather than something external. Developing this ability often involves trusting your instincts and learning to distinguish between everyday thoughts and spiritual communication. It's a personal, sometimes subtle, but deeply meaningful way to connect with the unseen.

CLAIRSENTIENCE, DESCRIBED AS "CLEAR FEELING" or "clear sensing," is the ability to pick up on energy, emotions, and sometimes even physical sensations from the surroundings, people, objects, or unseen spiritual entities, all without relying on the five common senses. This psychic sense fosters a deep, empathetic understanding, offering insights into situations or the emotions of others, and sometimes even the history of a place or object, simply by feeling it. Clairsentients might experience this as a gut instinct, physical sensations (like a sudden chill or warmth), or emotional impressions, which then guide their decisions or deepen their understanding of the energy around them.

. . .

CLAIRCOGNIZANCE, OR "CLEAR KNOWING," is when someone just knows something without any logical explanation as to how they came to that understanding. It's as if a piece of information or a realization about a person, place, event, or idea just drops into their mind out of nowhere, without any direct evidence or thought process. People with claircognizance might have these moments of insight spontaneously, feeling an undeniable certainty about the information they've received. This psychic ability is just one of several clairsenses that go beyond the normal human sensory experience.

BY RECOGNIZING and nurturing our intuition, we open ourselves up to new perspectives and experiences, gaining clarity in uncertain times and empowering us to trust our own inner wisdom. As we grow more in tune with this inner voice, we unlock a valuable ally in navigating the complexities of life.

ROLE OF GUARDIAN ANGELS AND SPIRIT GUIDES

Guardian angels and spirit guides play a pivotal role in our journey through life, serving as unseen protectors and advisors who guide us through the challenges and decisions we face. While they might not always make their presence known physically, their guidance can be felt in various ways, shaping our path and helping us grow spiritually.

Guardian angels are believed to be divine entities assigned to protect and guide us from birth until we transition from the physical world. Their primary role is to watch over us, offering comfort during distress and helping steer us away from harm's way. Many people report feeling a sense of warmth or a gentle nudge in the right direction during crucial moments, which they attribute to the loving presence of their guardian angel.

. . .

SPIRIT GUIDES, on the other hand, are often thought to be souls who have lived earthly lives and have now guided and mentored us from the spiritual realm. They can come from various backgrounds and may include ancestors, past life connections, or even historical figures who resonate with us deeply. Spirit guides are instrumental in helping us navigate our spiritual path, offering wisdom and insights gleaned from their experiences.

GUARDIAN ANGELS and spirit guides communicate with us subtly, often through signs, synchronicities, and intuition. You might notice a sudden idea or solution that comes out of nowhere, or you may experience recurring dreams that offer guidance on a particular issue. These are just a few ways in which our celestial allies make their presence felt, always working behind the scenes to support our highest good.

ENGAGING with our guardian angels and spirit guides can profoundly enrich our lives. By cultivating a relationship with them through meditation, prayer, or simply setting the intention to connect, we open ourselves up to their wisdom and guidance. This can lead to a deeper understanding of our life's purpose, enhanced intuition, and a stronger connection to the divine.

IN SHORT, guardian angels and spirit guides are invaluable companions on our spiritual journey, providing protection, guidance, and insight at every step. By acknowledging their presence and seeking to connect with them, we can unlock a deeper dimension of our spiritual practice and experience a more prosperous, more guided life journey.

ORIGIN OF ANGEL NUMBERS

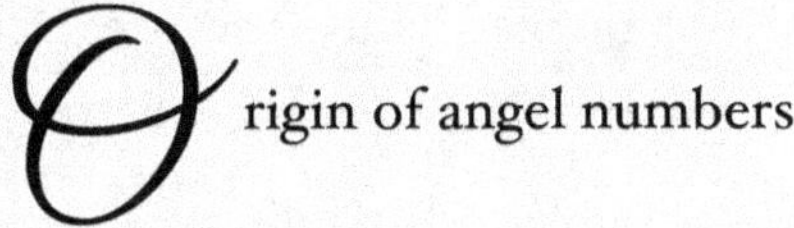rigin of angel numbers

ANGEL NUMBERS ARE GENUINELY CAPTIVATING, wouldn't you agree? They represent an ancient, mystical language shared across various cultures and spiritual traditions for centuries. Picture this: long before our era, civilizations such as those in Egypt and Babylon were already attuned to the unique energies of numbers, seeking insights from the cosmos. And then there was Pythagoras, the ingenious Greek philosopher, who elevated the entire concept. He distinctly perceived numbers, attributing specific energies and meanings to each. This marked the beginning of numerology as we know it.

. . .

When we discuss "angel numbers," we're delving into a somewhat more contemporary concept yet deeply rooted in those ancient teachings. It's the enchanting notion that angels or the cosmos communicate with us through numbers. Consider how often these sequences appear in our daily lives, be it on a clock, a license plate, or a receipt, with each sequence carrying a unique message meant just for us.

In many spiritual traditions, angels are viewed as messengers linking us to the divine. Thus, the idea of conveying messages through numbers is quite fitting. Numbers are universally understood; regardless of language, the number 3 remains the number 3.

What's intriguing is that decoding these numbers is highly individual. It's about what truly resonates within you. Typically, it's regarded as a positive and empowering method to engage with your spirituality and intuition. Encountering these sequences can feel like a reassuring nod from the cosmos, offering guidance, support, or simply affirming that you're on the right path.

WHAT ARE MASTER NUMBERS

Understanding Master Numbers in Numerology

MASTER NUMBERS ARE MORE than just figures in numerology; they carry a distinctive energy that can spark profound spiritual growth and personal evolution. Unlike typical numbers that are simplified down to a single digit, master numbers keep their original form due to their exceptional vibrations. The most recognized ones—11, 22, and 33—are known for their powerful traits, such as intuition, vision, and spiritual mastery. People who resonate with these master numbers often find themselves facing heightened responsibilities but also incredible chances to make a significant difference in the world.

. . .

MASTER NUMBER 11: The Intuitive Leader

OFTEN REFERRED to as the number of spiritual insight, 11 symbolizes heightened intuition and visionary leadership. Individuals who align with this number are typically very empathic, drawn to the mysteries of life, and on a quest for spiritual answers. As natural leaders, those embodying 11 energy possess a gift for foresight, enabling them to guide others in their spiritual journeys. However, this sensitivity can sometimes lead to anxiety or emotional overwhelm. With awareness and balance, those connected to 11 can unlock remarkable spiritual awakenings and empowerment.

MASTER NUMBER 22: The Master Builder

KNOWN AS THE "MASTER BUILDER," 22 reflects the energy of transforming grand dreams into reality. People resonating with this number have a remarkable knack for turning abstract ideas into solid outcomes. They blend practicality with spirituality, acting as a bridge between the physical and spiritual realms. Yet, along with great potential comes great responsibility. Those with 22's energy are encouraged to use their abilities for the greater good, aiming to create something lasting for themselves and others. Their journey often revolves around learning to harmonize ambition with humility and service.

MASTER NUMBER 33: The Master Teacher

MASTER NUMBER 33 embodies pure love, compassion, and selfless service, earning it the title of "Master Teacher." This number signifies a peak level of spiritual growth, and individuals influenced by 33 often feel called to heal, teach, and nurture others. Their life mission revolves around serving the collective, sometimes prioritizing others' needs over their own. The essence of 33 is a reminder of the crucial role love and kindness play in every endeavor. Yet, with such a weighty responsibility comes the risk of burnout, making it vital for those with this energy to also care for themselves.

CHALLENGES OF MASTER Numbers

WHILE MASTER NUMBERS come with immense potential, they also bring about significant challenges. The intensity of their energy can be quite a lot for those who are sensitive. It's not uncommon for individuals carrying master numbers to feel the weight of high expectations, both from themselves and the universe. This striving to live up to these powerful energies can lead to self-doubt and a sense of disconnection. It's important to remember that embracing master numbers isn't about achieving perfection; it's about growth and learning. They urge us to confront our limitations, face our fears, and evolve spiritually. Though the journey may be challenging, the rewards are plentiful when approached with mindfulness and self-compassion.

MASTER NUMBERS in Daily Life

YOU MIGHT FIND that master numbers sneak into your everyday life—through things like seeing 11:11 on a clock, spotting them on license plates passing by, or coming across significant dates. These occurrences aren't mere coincidences; they often act soft prompts from the universe, encouraging you to tune into its messages. If you keep seeing 11:11, for instance, it might be a signal for you to connect with your inner wisdom or hint at a spiritual awakening on the horizon. When these numbers pop up, pause and reflect on what guidance you might need in that moment. Master numbers can serve as invitations to delve deeper into your spiritual journey.

· · ·

The Role of Master Numbers in Personal Transformation

Engaging with master numbers can lead to genuine transformation in your life. They serve as powerful guides, helping you navigate your spiritual path and personal growth. By tuning into these numbers, you open yourself up to the opportunities and lessons they bring, illuminating your journey and inspiring you to embrace both the challenges and the blessings along the way.

The Role of Master Numbers in Personal Transformation

Master numbers hold a unique place in numerology, often discussed as powerful tools for personal growth and transformation. These numbers—11, 22, and 33—are believed to carry heightened energy and spiritual significance, offering deeper insights into our life paths.

When exploring master numbers, you might find that they resonate differently for each person. For instance, the number 11 is often seen as a symbol of intuition and enlightenment. If you keep encountering this number, it might consider it a gentle prompt to connect with your deeper insights and trust your instincts.

THE NUMBER 22, known as the Master Builder, is all about turning dreams into reality. It encourages ambition and practical steps toward your goals, making it a great ally for those looking to manifest their visions in tangible ways.

THEN THERE'S 33, often regarded as the Master Teacher, which emphasizes compassion and nurturing. It inspires you to share your knowledge and uplift others, making it a powerful force for transformation not just within yourself but for those around you.

UNDERSTANDING these master numbers can be a game changer on your personal journey. They invite you to look at where you are in life and challenge you to grow in ways you may not have considered before. Whether you're facing challenges or celebrating successes, these numbers can serve as guideposts, helping you navigate your path with purpose and clarity.

. . .

So, as you explore the meaning of these master numbers in your life, think about how they might resonate with your experiences and what transformations they might encourage. After all, personal transformation is often a journey, and having insightful tools at your disposal can make all the difference.

NUMEROLOGY

*N*ow, let's explore some of these numbers in detail.

NUMBER 1 SYMBOLIZES NEW BEGINNINGS, independence, and the power within you to shape your destiny. Encountering 1s frequently could prompt you to maintain a positive mindset, as your thoughts significantly influence reality.

NUMBER 2 EMBODIES BALANCE, harmony, and relationships. Finding 2s in your life could suggest it's time to value your connections or to remain patient, trusting in the emergence of the right partnerships.

. . .

NUMBER 3 REMINDS you to embrace your creativity and express yourself freely. It encourages you to savour the journey of personal growth and the joy of sharing your unique voice.

NUMBER 4 IS OFTEN ASSOCIATED with stability, practicality, and hard work. It reminds us that achieving our goals usually requires dedication and persistence. The energy of number 4 is grounding, encouraging us to build solid foundations for our dreams and aspirations. If you're encountering 4s frequently, it might be a sign to focus on creating a stable and secure environment for yourself and to trust in the power of perseverance.

NUMBER 5 SPEAKS TO CHANGE, adventure, and freedom. Its vibrant energy suggests significant trans-formations are on the horizon. Seeing 5s could indicate that it's time to embrace new experiences, be open to change, and adapt to the flow of life. This number encourages us to seek variety and be fearless in pursuing what makes us feel alive and excited.

NUMBER 6 IS DEEPLY CONNECTED to domestic harmony, responsibility, and care. It resonates with energies of compassion, nurturing, and family. When 6s start appearing in your life, it might be a call to focus on your home life, relationships, and responsibilities. It's a reminder to offer love and support to those around you and to ensure that you also care for your emotional well-being.

THE NUMBER 7 is known for its spiritual significance. It represents wisdom, introspection, and inner growth. This number invites us to look inward, encouraging deep contemplation and spiritual awakening. If you're seeing 7s, it could be a nudge to connect with your inner self, explore your spirituality, and trust in the intuitive insights from such exploration.

NUMBER 8 SYMBOLIZES ABUNDANCE, success, and achievement. It's a powerful energy that suggests the manifestation of material and spiritual wealth. Encountering 8s might signify that prosperity is within reach, provided you align your actions and mindset with your goals. It's also a reminder of the importance of balance between the material and spiritual realms, highlighting the concept of karma and the universal principle of cause and effect.

REACHING NUMBER 9, we touch upon themes of conclusion, universal love, and the importance of releasing what no longer benefits you to make space for new experiences.

EACH NUMBER CARRIES its unique message and energy, contributing to the broader spectrum of guidance offered by angel numbers and numerology. Whether it's a call to action, a reminder of your spiritual path, or an affirmation of your current journey, these numbers serve as markers along your personal and spiritual development, reinforcing that the universe is intricately connected to our individual experiences.

NOW, as I glance at the clock and see 5:55 - let's dive into what it means to see these numbers repeated as "angel numbers."

Angel number 000 is a profound signal, embodying the endless potential and marking the start of a significant spiritual journey. It reinforces our deep bond with the divine, highlighting our unity with the universe and its infinite energies. This number signals new beginnings and a wealth of opportunities ahead. It encourages embracing the endless possibilities before us, urging trust in the universe's flow and the perfect timing of our lives.

REPRESENTING a call to spiritual growth and a deeper cosmic understanding, 000 reminds us that the universe supports our quest for enlightenment, personal development, and realizing our soul's true purpose. It nudges us to listen to our intuition and divine guidance, steering us towards our greatest good.

. . .

IN NUMEROLOGY, 0 symbolizes completeness, eternity, and the start of a spiritual journey, emphasizing cycles, energy flow, and continual evolution. Tripled in 000, its meaning intensifies, suggesting unlimited potential, the origin of all creation, and a return to our true essence.

000 ENCOURAGES us to shed fears or limitations that hinder our full potential. It reminds us that every moment is a chance for a new beginning, inviting us to redefine ourselves and align with our divine mission. This number calls for making choices aligned with our highest selves and taking actions that mirror our natural desires.

ENCOUNTERING angel number 000 is a beautiful affirmation of divine love and support. It assures us we're never alone and that the universe guides us towards fulfilling our potential and leading purposeful lives. It's a symbol of encouragement, pushing us to embrace our spiritual path confidently and look forward to the journey with optimism and an open heart.

ANGEL NUMBER 000 is an inspiring message of endless possibilities, divine backing, and the thrilling onset of a deep spiritual quest. It invites us to recognize our potential, connect profoundly with the universe, and embark on self-discovery and spiritual awakening. It guides us towards a fuller understanding of ourselves and the universe and encourages an enthusiastic embrace of the journey of growth and enlightenment.

111

Whenever I see the number 111, it feels like a meaningful sign, like my thoughts are entirely in sync with the path I'm meant to be on. There's something profoundly spiritual and compelling about this number. In numerology, the number 1 is all about new starts, asserting your uniqueness, and the magic of making things happen and manifesting. When you triplicate that to 111, those meanings get supercharged – a triple dose of energy and possibility. This makes 111 unique, and it's a cousin to the sequence 1111, which is a whole other story.

I LIKE to think of 111 as a friendly nudge from the universe, telling me that my thoughts are in perfect harmony with the world around me. It's like a sign that the things I'm hoping and dreaming for aren't just fantasies; they're starting to happen. This sequence reminds me to keep my vibes positive and hopeful because the energy I put out is what I will get back.

SEEING 111 also makes me pause and reflect. It reminds me of how powerful our thoughts are in shaping our reality. The idea that we can shape our experiences and the world around us with our thoughts and desires is fascinating and empowering. It's a nudge to align our thoughts with what we genuinely want, believing we can bring our dreams to life.

I HOLD dear the concept of creating our reality with our thoughts. It ties in with the belief that we're the architects of our destiny and that the universe is cheering us on every step of the way. The number 111 is like a little sign from the universe, confirming that I'm on the right path, especially when I'm about to start something new or need a bit of reassurance.

I WITNESSED the creation of your reality through manifestation while with my mother. We were riding in the elevator in her apartment building with her sweet and loving dog, who can also be reactive to other dogs. On the way up, she kept repeating, "Please don't be dogs...Please don't be dogs..." The universe, I advised her, doesn't register words like "don't" or "no," so what my mother was asking for was, "Please, more dogs!" When the elevator door opened, low and behold, there was a dog. We continued to our floor, and there it appeared, as if by magic. Another two dogs. As we round the corner to approach her apartment...you guessed it. Another dog came out of a neighbouring apartment. So, a gentle suggestion is to be mindful of your words about yourself and others, as they hold significant power in creating your reality.

THE SIGNIFICANCE of the angel number III lies in its powerful reminder of our spiritual path. It serves as a gentle nudge from the universe, guiding and supporting us as we navigate our lives. It highlights how numbers can influence our thoughts and awareness of our spiritual journey.

222

Angel number 222 is a significant sign about trusting your journey and balancing everything. It's like the universe's way of nudging you toward finding a sweet spot between what you think, do, and feel. You might come across this number when you're at a turning point, Dealing with some challenging situations., or feeling unsure about what's ahead. It's a comforting reminder that things are moving as they should, even if not apparent.

ONE BIG THING 222 is trying to tell us is to find balance. It's like when you're juggling too much—work, relationships, taking care of yourself—and you start feeling all over the place. Seeing 222 is like getting a gentle push to slow down and find a way to bring peace and order back into your life. That way, you're better positioned to tackle challenges and make choices that align with your long-term goals.

ANGEL NUMBER 222 resonates deeply with the concept of harmony, emphasizing the significance of fostering amicable relationships. This number is a gentle reminder of the importance of our connections with friends, partners, and colleagues. It encourages us to be more open, genuinely engage with others, and cultivate bonds anchored in mutual trust and support. Moreover, when faced with disagreements or misunderstandings, 222 is a prompt to approach these situations with empathy and patience. It underscores the potential to achieve unity and understanding, suggesting that finding common ground is desirable and achievable.

ANGEL NUMBER 222 holds significant spiritual symbolism, emphasizing the importance of patience and faith in the unfolding of life's journey. It gently reminds us that, though we may crave quicker progress, there's a more profound wisdom in allowing events to unfold at their own pace. This number carries the message that unseen forces are at work, orchestrating the alignment of our endeavours—be it in our professional pursuits, personal relationships, or our path of self-discovery. It assures us that our efforts are gradually bearing fruit, and the rewards of our dedication will soon be evident. Angel number 222 serves as a beacon, indicating that we are aligned with our spiritual path and encouraging us to trust in the process, even when the end goal isn't in sight.

IN THE WORLD OF NUMEROLOGY, the number 2 is all about balance, being open, and sensitivity, and when you see it tripled as 222, it's like these energies are supercharged. The universe reminds us to balance our inner thoughts and the outer world, stay positive, and listen to our gut feelings. It's a nudge to trust that if we remain true to ourselves and act honestly, everything will work out as it should.

So, angel number 222 is a big, comforting hug from the universe, telling us to keep the faith, aim for balance, and cherish our connections. It's a reminder that support is all around us, and by staying focused on what's truly important, we're setting ourselves up for some positive changes. Whether going through a rough patch or just seeking reassurance, 222 is a sign that good things are coming, and all that patience and hard work will be worth it.

333

*E*ncountering the number 333 repeatedly in your life signifies more than mere coincidence—it's an exhilarating nod from the universe, confirming you're heading in the right direction. This number acts as a cosmic hug, ensuring that all necessary support and guidance to reach your potential is within reach, courtesy of angels, spiritual mentors or guides, or the universe itself. Knowing such formidable allies are in your corner is genuinely heartening.

WHEN 333 APPEARS, it signals that you're perfectly aligned with the universe's rhythm, indicating full steam ahead on your chosen path. This isn't a random occurrence; it encourages persistence because your efforts are paying off.

. . .

AT ITS CORE, 333 signifies spiritual evolution, often surfacing as you reach significant spiritual landmarks—whether it's gaining profound universal insights, deepening your spiritual connection, or discovering your true calling. It reassures you to welcome these transformations, affirming you're on the correct trajectory. This number is also associated with the holistic balance of body, mind, and spirit, underscoring its spiritual essence.

FROM A NUMEROLOGICAL PERSPECTIVE, the essence of the number 3 revolves around creativity, authentic communication, and self-expression. Thus, encountering 333 serves as a motivational speech to ignite your imagination. It's the universe's way of saying it's time to launch new ventures, find your voice, or share your talents without hesitation.

ADDITIONALLY, 333 emphasizes authenticity—staying true to oneself and openly expressing one's truth in various life aspects. It reassures you that the universe supports your genuine self.

IF YOU EVER FEEL ISOLATED, seeing 333 is a comforting reminder that you're well-supported. It signifies that a network of love, including the universe, angels, and spiritual guides, has your back, offering reassurance that you're on the right path and divine assistance is at hand.

FURTHERMORE, 333 encourages a holistic equilibrium—aligning mind, body, and spirit if life seems unbalanced. It's the universe's way of highlighting the power of positivity and manifestation, motivating you to stay focused on your aspirations with optimism and resilience as you advance toward your goals.

444

Angel number 444 symbolizes stability, protection, and divine reassurance. It marks the presence of angels and spiritual guides, offering support and guidance in every aspect of life—relationships, careers, personal growth, and spiritual paths.

Seeing 444 indicates that you're never alone, especially in challenging times. It reminds you of divine support, urging you to remain grounded and trust in this guidance. The number emphasizes the importance of building solid and lasting foundations for success.

In numerology, 4 signifies stability, practicality, and order. The repetition in 444 amplifies these qualities, encouraging methodical, diligent efforts toward your goals. It calls for balance across all life facets, urging harmony between work, rest, and personal growth. This balance supports a grounded, holistic lifestyle.

ADDITIONALLY, 444 underscores the need to trust your journey, even when faced with obstacles or uncertainties. It's a sign that you're aligned with your higher purpose, and everything will fall into place in time. This number also signals a phase of manifestation, indicating that your efforts are close to bearing fruit.

ULTIMATELY, 444 is a motivational message to take action toward building the life you desire. It reminds you that divine forces are supporting you every step of the way. It encourages divine support and personal dedication to achieving long-term success and stability.

555

*A*ngel number 555 is a potent symbol of transformation. It represents the tremendous changes that are taking place in your life, signalling the start of a new and exciting chapter that is brimming with opportunities for personal growth and alignment with your higher purpose. This number indicates that significant change is on the horizon or is already underway.

IT ENCOURAGES you to release anything that no longer serves your highest good gracefully and remain open to the abundance of new possibilities coming your way. At its core, 555 embodies the essence of freedom, urging you to embrace your true self and follow a path that truly resonates with your soul's purpose.

. . .

DESPITE THE NATURAL apprehensions accompanying change, Angel 555 wants you to know you are fully supported. It inspires you to let go of fear and resistance and believe in your journey's beautiful unfolding.
80

ABOVE ALL, 555 serves as a reminder of your incredible ability to manifest positive changes in your life through maintaining a positive mindset and setting clear intentions. Embrace this remarkable journey and step boldly into the fantastic new chapter that awaits you!

666

The number 666 is often misunderstood and wrongly associated with negativity, but in the context of angel numbers, it holds a positive and spiritually significant meaning. It is a message from the universe urging us to seek balance, engage in self-reflection, and align ourselves with our higher purpose. When we encounter angel number 666, it is a gentle reminder to bring balance into our lives, realign our focus, and prioritize inner peace and fulfillment. This number prompts us to release limiting thoughts, trust the universe, and shift our mindset to positivity and gratitude.

ANGEL NUMBER 666 signifies the need to concentrate on what brings us inner peace and fulfillment, nurture ourselves and those around us, and find a balance between our material needs and spiritual growth. It encourages us to release negative thinking, fears, and insecurities and instead focus on love, peace, and abundance. Encountering 666 also signifies that we are on the brink of spiritual awakening and are called to deepen our connection with our higher selves.

THIS NUMBER IS ASSOCIATED with reassessing the direction of our lives, focusing on spiritual development, nurturing meaningful relationships, and showing compassion and kindness to others. It also carries a message about manifesting abundance in our lives by staying grounded, focused, and aligned with our higher purpose. Angel number 666 is a powerful message of balance, self-reflection, and spiritual growth. It encourages us to embrace its deeper, positive meaning and focus on harmony.

*A*ngel number 777 symbolizes a deep spiritual connection, inner wisdom, and enlightenment. It stands out as a positive beacon, indicating that we are on the right path and encouraging us to continue our pursuit of knowledge, understanding, and personal growth. This number is a reminder from the universe and the angels that our efforts toward spiritual enlightenment are recognized and supported.

ENCOUNTERING 777 invites us to introspection and self-discovery, especially when questioning our life's purpose. It encourages trusting our intuition and exploring our inner depths to connect with our authentic selves. In numerology, seven is associated with the spiritual realm and introspection; thus, 777 amplifies these qualities, signalling accelerated spiritual growth, heightened psychic awareness, and an invitation to embark on a spiritual quest.

ANGEL NUMBER 777 also urges us to embrace our uniqueness and spiritual gifts, suggesting that now is the time to develop and use these abilities for the highest good. It signifies alignment with the universal energies and that our thoughts, actions, and intentions are harmoniously connected with our soul's purpose, bringing opportunities that resonate deeply with us.

MOREOVER, 777 highlights the importance of awareness of the synchronicities and signs from the universe, encouraging us to pay attention to subtle messages and guidance. It emphasizes lifelong learning and personal development through reading, meditation, workshops, or spiritual practices.

OVERALL, angel number 777 carries a powerful message of spiritual enlightenment, trust in our journey, and the joy of aligning with our highest selves, supported by divine guidance and encouragement. It opens us to spiritual discovery, deeper understanding, and a richer connection with the divine.

888

*A*ngel number 888 emerges as a potent emblem of abundance, equilibrium, and the rewards of karma, echoing the universal principle of causality. It radiates with a message of positivity and assurance from the cosmos, signalling that all manners of prosperity are within our reach. This numeral stands as a compelling signal that we are aligned with the path to financial solidity and tangible achievements, contingent on our commitment to maintaining harmony and balance in our endeavours.

THE ENCOUNTER with angel number 888 stimulates us to adopt a positive outlook, remain dedicated to our objectives, and have faith that our endeavours will yield significant returns. This symbol heralds financial growth and career advancement, indicating that our diligent efforts are on the verge of culminating in remarkable rewards.

IN NUMEROLOGY, the digit eight is synonymous with abundance, authority, and wealth creation. The amplification effect of this number when it appears thrice, as in 888, magnifies its influence, denoting a phase of potent manifestation where our thoughts and deeds have a pronounced impact on our reality. It calls for aligning our intentions and actions with the greater good, ensuring that our manifestations contribute positively to ourselves and others.

FURTHERMORE, angel number 888 underscores the significance of balance in our quest for achievement. It reminds us that true prosperity transcends material gains and encompasses emotional, spiritual, and relational wellness. This numeral encourages us to seek equilibrium in all facets of life, guaranteeing that our success journey does not compromise our health, relationships, or personal development.

ADDITIONALLY, 888 signifies universal support for our ventures, indicating a harmonious cycle of giving and receiving. It affirms that our positive deeds, generosity, and hard work will be met with equivalent reciprocation. This number embodies the principle that our contributions to the universe will return to us manifold.

THE APPEARANCE of 888 also encourages us to embrace our intrinsic power and take decisive steps toward our aspirations. It reminds us of our capacity to mould our fate through our perspectives, convictions, and actions. The angels encourage us to wield our power, make courageous choices, and have confidence in the co-creation process with the cosmos.

THIS NUMBER ACCENTUATES the theme of karmic equilibrium, reminding us that our actions bear consequences and that living with integrity, cultivating gratitude, and practicing generosity will lead to favourable outcomes. It urges us to align with our utmost truths and act compassionately and kindly.

IN ESSENCE, angel number 888 conveys a message of encouragement, prosperity, and karmic recompense. It reassures us of the universe's bounty and its sufficiency for everyone. By harmonizing our actions with our loftiest aims and maintaining balance in our lives, we can draw the affluence and success we seek. The manifestation 888 is a comforting indication of cosmic support in our pursuit of dreams, urging us to stay optimistic, engage in inspired action, and trust in the universe's abundance.

999

*A*ngel number 999 marks a momentous turning point, foreshadowing the end of one chapter and the start of another, brimming with promise and new beginnings. This number is a profound signal, urging us to confidently embrace the changes ahead and trust in the journey the universe has laid out for us. It's a reminder to let go of fears or doubts and believe these transitions guide us toward our best possible futures.

SEEING 999 is like receiving a wise nudge to prepare for significant changes that will ultimately align with our deepest purposes. It emphasizes the importance of closing old doors to make way for new opportunities, encouraging us to shed any baggage holding us back.

. . .

IN NUMEROLOGY, the number nine symbolizes wisdom, karma, and the fulfillment of goals. It also stands for altruism and setting a positive example for others. The triple occurrence of this number, as in 999, amplifies its influence, urging us to live authentically and pursue our spiritual destinies with total commitment.

MOREOVER, 999 calls upon us to reflect on how we can contribute to humanity's betterment, utilizing our unique gifts to make a lasting impact. It's a beautiful reminder that by helping others, we fulfill our soul's mission and play a part in the collective good.

THIS NUMBER also prompts us to focus on personal growth and spiritual development, seeking experiences that enrich our spirits and deepen our self-awareness. It reassures us of angelic support in our quest for wisdom and self-discovery.

ENCOUNTERING 999 SIGNALS, it's time to release anything that doesn't serve our highest good, such as outdated beliefs, toxic relationships, or harmful habits. Letting go opens us up to positive energy and new possibilities.

. . .

IN ESSENCE, angel number 999 is a message filled with hope, encouragement, and divine guidance. It reassures us that we're on the right path, with everything unfolding as part of a grand, divine plan. It invites us to look ahead with optimism, ready to embark on a fulfilling journey that resonates deeply with our soul's mission.

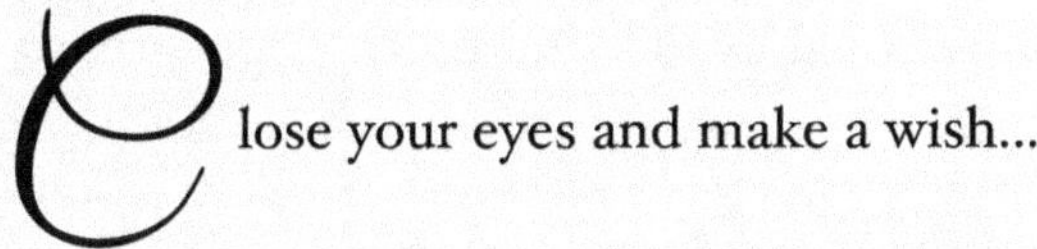

Close your eyes and make a wish...

ANGEL NUMBER 1111 signifies a potent and spiritually significant message from the universe, heralding a gateway to new beginnings and opportunities for personal growth. It symbolizes intuition, spiritual awakening, and enlightenment, urging us to connect deeply with our inner thoughts and feelings. The appearance of 1111 reminds us of the immense power of our thoughts, encouraging us to manifest our deepest desires into reality by maintaining a positive mindset.

THIS NUMBER SEQUENCE invites us to courageously pursue our dreams and goals, serving as a wake-up call to discover our true purpose and align with our soul's mission. It prompts us to be mindful of our thoughts and emotions, guiding us toward fulfilling our life's direction.

IN NUMEROLOGY, 1 represents new beginnings, independence, and the ability to create our reality. When amplified as 1111, its significance is greatly magnified, symbolizing spiritual awakening and the discovery of our power. This serves as a signal from the universe for accelerated personal evolution and the opportunity to enact significant changes in our lives.

ENCOUNTERING 1111 also reminds us to remain open to the universe's guidance and support, trusting our intuition and inner wisdom to lead us toward joy and fulfillment. It encourages a positive outlook and focuses on our highest aspirations, assuring us of the universe's support in achieving our goals.

THE NUMBER 1111 holds powerful significance, especially with the double master number 11 embedded within it. In numerology, 11 is considered a master number, symbolizing intuition, spiritual awakening, and enlightenment. When you see 1111, it's like a cosmic nudge, a reminder that you're aligned with your higher purpose or entering a phase of personal growth. The double 11 amplifies this energy, suggesting that you're in a unique position to manifest your desires and tap into your inner wisdom. It's often seen as a sign that the universe is supporting your spiritual journey, encouraging you to follow your intuition and keep to the path that feels most authentic.

FURTHERMORE, seeing 1111 indicates that we are on the right path, with our thoughts and actions paving the way for realizing our desires. It inspires us to embrace individuality and authenticity, attracting favourable circumstances and people into our lives.

IN SUMMARY, encountering angel number 1111 is an uplifting and affirming experience, signalling that the universe supports and guides us. It is a call to embrace our spiritual journey, believe in our potential, and trust in life's journey. It reminds us of our power to manifest our dreams and live according to our soul's purpose.

1010

*A*ngel number 1010 is a powerful message from the universe, signalling that you're amid a spiritual awakening or significant personal growth. It combines the energies of 1 and 0, each repeated twice, amplifying their influence. To truly understand what 1010 means for you, it's essential to look at the individual components of the number and the overarching message they deliver when combined.

THE NUMBER 1 in numerology represents new beginnings, leadership, self-confidence, and the ability to create your reality. When you see this number, it's often a reminder that you have the power within you to manifest your desires and shape the path ahead. The number 0, conversely, signifies potential, wholeness, and the start of a spiritual journey. It often symbolizes the energy of the universe itself—something vast, infinite, and full of possibility. When 0 appears, it acts as a magnifier for the numbers it appears with, intensifying their energy.

WHEN YOU COMBINE these meanings in 1010, the number becomes a message of alignment and encouragement. The universe is nudging you to pay attention to your spiritual growth, recognize that you are on the right path, and trust that the opportunities ahead align with your soul's purpose.

ANGEL NUMBER 1010 is often seen during times of transformation or when you're entering a new phase in life. This number serves as a reminder that you are evolving spiritually and personally. It's not just about change, though—it's about conscious growth. The number encourages you to stay focused on your spiritual path, to trust the process, and to remain positive even when things seem uncertain. The repetition of 1 and 0 suggests that the universe supports you, and you're being guided to keep moving forward with faith in your intuition.

IF YOU'VE BEEN FEELING stuck or unsure of your next steps, 1010 is a signal to trust in the divine timing of your life. The universe is reminding you that everything is unfolding as it should, even if it doesn't feel that way right now. It's an invitation to lean into the flow of life, releasing the need for control and allowing the natural rhythm of the universe to guide you.

ONE OF THE core messages of angel number 1010 is empowerment. It's a gentle push to embrace your strength and capability. You have everything you need to manifest your dreams, and the time to take action is now. The number 1 encourages you to be proactive and take charge of your life, while the 0 amplifies this message by reminding you of the infinite possibilities that lie before you. When you see 1010, it's the universe telling you that now is the time to take bold steps toward your goals, knowing that divine forces fully support you.

BUT EMPOWERMENT DOESN'T JUST MEAN TAKING action. It also means taking responsibility for your energy, your thoughts, and your mindset. 1010 asks you to be mindful of what you're focusing on because your thoughts are incredibly powerful right now. Positive thinking, affirmations, and visualization techniques can help you align with desired outcomes. You are co-creating your reality, and the universe is urging you to step fully into this role with confidence and clarity.

. . .

ANOTHER VITAL MESSAGE behind angel number 1010 is trust—trusting yourself and the universe. Life may throw unexpected challenges, but seeing 1010 reminds you that you are exactly where you need to be. Even if the path ahead seems unclear, this number encourages you to have faith in the process. It's about trusting that every experience is helping you grow and evolve, even the difficult ones.

IF YOU'VE BEEN second-guessing your decisions or feeling unsure about a particular direction, 1010 offers reassurance. You are being guided, and things will unfold in their own time. This is a moment to practice patience and allow things to happen naturally. While taking action when needed is essential, releasing the need for immediate results is equally important. Trust that the universe is working behind the scenes, aligning the pieces of your life in ways that you may not yet fully understand.

ANOTHER LAYER of 1010's meaning relates to balance—particularly between your material desires and spiritual growth. The number 1 focuses on achieving personal goals, success, and self-advancement, while the number 0 speaks to spiritual oneness and higher consciousness.

Together, these numbers remind you that it's important to nurture both aspects of your life.

THIS COULD BE a time to evaluate how much energy you put into your material success versus your spiritual well-being. Are you too focused on external achievements, neglecting your inner self? Or, conversely, are you so caught up in your spiritual practice that you're not taking steps to fulfill your personal goals? Angel number 1010 is a reminder to seek harmony between these two realms. True fulfillment comes from balancing both the practical and the spiritual aspects of life.

IN ESSENCE, angel number 1010 is a signal of forward movement. You are being asked to trust in your journey and keep pushing ahead with confidence, knowing that the universe is supporting you every step of the way. The repeating 1's are a sign that you are creating your reality, and the repeating 0's indicate that you're divinely guided. Whether you're about to start a new project, deepen a relationship, or explore a new spiritual practice, 1010 reminds you that now is the time to act.

PLEASE TAKE it as a sign to release self-doubt and embrace the opportunities before you. You are not alone on this journey—the universe is walking with you, guiding you toward your highest good. The appearance of 1010 is a powerful message that you're aligned with your purpose, and everything is unfolding in perfect timing. Keep your thoughts positive, open to new possibilities, and trust your strength to bring your visions to life.

1212

ngel number 1212 signals a decisive moment of balance and alignment in your life, pointing you toward a phase of personal growth and harmony. This sequence suggests you're on the verge of a significant transformation, urging you to stay aligned with your deepest beliefs and intentions.

THE NUMBER 1 speaks to leadership, assertiveness, and the potential for new adventures. The number 2, meanwhile, represents harmony, cooperation, and the importance of nurturing connections. Together, they form a symphony of positivity, encouraging you to keep a balanced outlook as you pursue your dreams and face challenges.

. . .

SEEING 1212 reminds you to trust your journey, affirming that your desires are within reach. It's a nudge to maintain faith and work diligently towards your goals, with the universe supporting your efforts to manifest your aspirations.

ADDITIONALLY, 1212 emphasizes the value of open-heartedness in giving and receiving love and support, highlighting the interconnectedness of our relationships and their role in our growth and mutual support.

REGARDING MANIFESTING YOUR DREAMS, 1212 serves as a motivational beacon, urging you to align your thoughts with your highest goals. This alignment attracts the positive energies needed to make your dreams a reality. It often appears when you need a confidence boost or a reminder that the universe is on your side, encouraging you to proceed with optimism.

THE NUMBER also underscores the importance of being attentive to your environment and the people you meet, who may offer insights or help that align with your spiritual path. It calls for embracing change and adaptability, assuring you that these transitions will lead to greater harmony and fulfillment.

. . .

Beyond its immediate message, 1212 invites you to deepen your spiritual exploration through meditation, prayer, or other spiritual practices. This deepening connection offers clarity, inner peace, and a better understanding of your life's purpose and lessons.

In summary, angel number 1212 is a profoundly positive sign, confirming you're on the right path spiritually and in daily life. It encourages focus, balance, and openness to the boundless opportunities ahead. The significance of 1212 may vary for each person, so reflect on how it resonates with your journey and guides you toward your highest good.

WHAT ARE PATTERN NUMBERS?

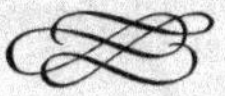

*I*n the fascinating world of numerology, specific number sequences—like 2234, 234, 456, or 987—carry unique meanings, much like angel numbers or those intriguing repeating digits we often encounter. Many believe these patterns are messages from the universe, guiding us on our personal and spiritual journeys. While angel numbers typically emphasize individual digits or repetitions, pattern numbers add another layer by featuring sequences or mirrored structures, each with its significance.

UNDERSTANDING PATTERN NUMBERS

PATTERNS IN NUMBERS often symbolize growth, movement, and cycles in our lives. Take sequence 234, for instance—it represents a steady advancement, signifying that you're on the right path and steadily progressing toward your goals. On the other hand, something like 456 suggests a burst of growth or a nudge to take action. These numbers gently remind us that life is a continuous journey, and we play an essential role in this evolution.

MOREOVER, pattern numbers can highlight areas that may need balance or re-evaluation. The sequence 987, for example, signifies that you might be concluding a chapter in your life, urging you to prepare for fresh starts or to release what no longer serves you. When you notice these patterns pop up repeatedly, please take a moment to reflect on your life's circumstances; they're often nudging you toward context-specific insights.

A QUICK LOOK at Some Common Pattern Numbers

2234: This number serves as a reminder of balance and harmony, indicating that you're finding equilibrium in various aspects of your life. It encourages you to stay on this balanced path, reassuring you that you're building a solid foundation for future success.

234: Representing a journey of steady progress, 234 signals that you are on the right track. It suggests that your efforts are being noticed, reinforcing that your path aligns with your aspirations.

456: This sequence symbolizes energetic growth and forward movement. It's a call to embrace change and step boldly into new opportunities. The essence of 456 is about taking decisive action, knowing that those choices lead to meaningful personal development.

987: This number often symbolizes completion. It suggests that you're about to finish a significant phase in your life. It's a moment for reflection and preparation for new adventures, indicating that you're ready to move on from your current situation.

MORE INSIGHTS AWAIT

DIVING DEEPER into pattern numbers reveals a captivating mix of numerology and spiritual insight. Each sequence carries messages that extend far beyond mere digits, prompting us to reflect on our life journeys. Whether they signify progress, action, or completion, pattern numbers are powerful tools for understanding where we stand and where we might be headed.

STAY TUNED as we explore even more about how to interpret these impactful numerical patterns! There's much more to uncover, and with each discovery, we can gain further clarity on the messages the universe is sending our way.

WHAT TO DO WHEN YOU ENCOUNTER ANGEL NUMBERS

Encountering angel numbers is an incredible opportunity to gain insights and guidance from the universe. When you come across these numbers, you can connect with a higher power and receive messages uniquely tailored to you. Here's a positive and empowering guide on what to do when you encounter angel numbers:

EMBRACE THE NUMBER: When encountering an angel number, embrace it with excitement and curiosity. Each number or sequence holds a particular vibration and message meant just for you.

REFLECT ON YOUR LIFE: Take a moment to reflect on your current life situation. Angel numbers often provide guidance or reassurance related to what's happening in your life, your thoughts, or your questions.

DISCOVER THE MEANING: Every angel number has a general meaning but also contains a personal message. Research the significance of the number and interpret its message in the context of your life and experiences.

IDENTIFY SPECIFIC ASPECTS: Angel numbers can illuminate specific areas of your life, such as your career, relationships, or personal growth. Pay attention to whether the number points toward a particular aspect or theme.

TRUST YOUR INTUITION: Your intuition is a powerful tool for understanding the message behind angel numbers. Once familiar with their general meanings, trust your instincts to lead you to a personal interpretation.

TAKE INSPIRED ACTION: If the message resonates with you, consider what inspired actions you can take to align more closely with the guidance you've received. This might involve making positive changes, pursuing new opportunities, or focusing on personal growth.

. . .

EXPRESS GRATITUDE: Thank the angel numbers for their guidance and reassurance. Expressing gratitude can open your heart to receive further messages and blessings.

REMAIN OPEN-MINDED: Stay open to receiving additional messages from the universe. Angel numbers can appear in various forms and at different times, providing ongoing guidance and support.

JOURNAL YOUR EXPERIENCES: Journaling when and where you encounter angel numbers, along with your thoughts, feelings, and the circumstances at the time, can deepen your understanding of their significance in your life.

SHARE YOUR EXPERIENCES: Sharing your experiences with angel numbers with others can be enlightening and enriching. It can offer different perspectives on the messages and affirm the guidance you're receiving.

. . .

REMEMBER, encountering angel numbers is a profoundly personal and spiritual experience. The most crucial aspect is what they mean to you and how they can guide you toward greater wisdom, happiness, and fulfillment. Embrace this journey with positivity and openness, and you'll be amazed by the insights and blessings that come your way.

CONCLUSION

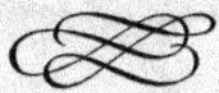

In wrapping up, delving into the study of angel numbers uncovers an incredibly captivating and rewarding dimension of spiritual guidance and universal communication. It provides a remarkable perspective through which we can understand and interpret the universe's signs and messages. By immersing ourselves in the intricate language of numbers, we gain a deeper insight into our life's purpose, innermost aspirations, and spiritual odyssey. Each number, with its unique vibration and significance, serves as a guiding light—offering support, solace, and motivation as we navigate the intricacies of our existence.

WE HAVE STRIVED to unravel the enchanting tapestry of numbers, equipping readers with the means to decipher the divine messages surrounding us, waiting to be unveiled. As we conclude this chapter on angel numbers, we hope to leave you, our dear readers, feeling empowered to attune yourselves more closely to the universe's whispers, to trust deeply in the profound guidance it offers, and to embark on your journey towards your truest selves with open hearts and a renewed sense of wonder. Always remember, the universe constantly communicates with us; it's our responsibility to tune in, interpret its wisdom, and allow it to illuminate the path ahead.

ABOUT THE AUTHOR

Steven W. Watson is a spiritual writer with a deep passion for exploring the mysteries of the universe. His work decodes the hidden meanings behind numbers and symbols, helping readers find clarity and guidance on their journeys. With a thoughtful approach, Steven shares insights into the spiritual connections that shape our lives, offering wisdom that resonates with those seeking a deeper understanding of the world around them. Through his writings, he aims to inspire others to discover their paths of enlightenment and growth.

Growing up on the west coast of Canada in British Columbia, Steven has often contemplated the meanings of life and our place in the universe. He finds great solace in exploring spiritual communities and realms to uncover deeper insights. Steven firmly believes that we are the creators of our lives through the art of manifestation and co-creation with the universe. After years of exploration, meditation, and connection with the universe, he considers himself a spiritual individual eager to share his insights into the wonders of existence.

In addition to his spiritual writings, Steven has also written romance novels that will soon be released, such as the first book of the series, **Fates Entwined**, with book 1 - ***Threads of Fate***. As a proud member of the LGBT+ community, Steven focuses on LGBT+ writings and heart-wrenching romances for all to enjoy.

Follow his journey through his extensive writings by visiting www.enlightenedflame.com to subscribe to the mailing list for future works of fiction and non-fiction.

Please also feel free to leave your review on our Amazon page about how you enjoyed this book!

With a heart full of gratitude - we hope you enjoyed this book. We are looking forward to our subsequent encounter.

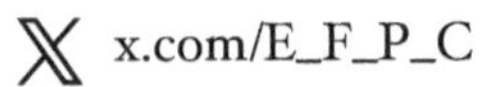